My Ride with Glory

NELSON HARDY

WestBow
PRESS
A DIVISION OF THOMAS NELSON

WestBow Press books may be ordered through booksellers or by contacting:

WestBow Press
A Division of Thomas Nelson
1663 Liberty Drive
Bloomington, IN 47403
www.westbowpress.com
1-(866) 928-1240

Because of the dynamic nature of the Internet, any web addresses or
links contained in this book may have changed since publication and
may no longer be valid. The views expressed in this work are solely those
of the author and do not necessarily reflect the views of the publisher,
and the publisher hereby disclaims any responsibility for them.

Any people depicted in stock imagery provided by Thinkstock are
models, and such images are being used for illustrative purposes only.

Certain stock imagery © Thinkstock.

ISBN: 978-1-4497-8735-6 (sc)
ISBN: 978-1-4497-8736-3 (hc)
ISBN: 978-1-4497-8733-2 (e)

Library of Congress Control Number: 2013904165

Printed in the United States of America

WestBow Press rev. date: 4/02/2013

TABLE OF CONTENTS

Acknowledgements ix

Preface 1

Introduction 3

Easter 2009 6

July 10, 2011 23

July 11, 2011 24

July 14, 2011 24

July 15, 2011 24

July 17, 2011 26

July 19, 2011 26

July 20, 2011 26

July 21, 2011 27

July 22, 2011 27

July 23, 2011 27

July 24, 2011 28

July 26, 2011 28

July 27, 2011 30

August 1, 2011 32

August 3, 2011 35

August 5, 2011 35

August 7, 2011 35

August 10, 2011 36

August 12, 2011 36

August 17, 2011 37

August 24, 2011 37

August 29, 2011 38

September 6, 2011 38

September 7, 2011 38

September 8, 2011 39

September 9, 2011 39

September 10, 2011 39

September 13, 2011 40

September 18, 2011 40

September 23, 2011 41

September 28, 2011 41

October 13, 2011 43

October 15, 2011 45

November 21, 2011 46

November 24, 2011 48

November 26, 2011 48

November 27, 2011 49

December 1, 2011 49

December 5, 2011 50

December 7, 2011 50

December 9, 2011 51

February 28, 2012 51

March 11, 2012 53

March 13, 2012 54

March 14, 2012 54

March 16, 2012 55

March 22, 2012 55

March 23, 2012 56

March 24, 2012 59

March 31, to April 8, 2012 61

April 21, 2012 63

April 24, 2012 63

April 26, 2012, ... 65

April 30, 2012 66

May 2, 2012 66

May 17, 2012 67

May 21, 2012 67

July 17, 2012 72

September 22, 2012 73

October 2, 2012 74

October 24, 2012 75

November 6, 2012 75

November 7, 2012 76

November 9, 2012 78

November 10, 2012 80

Discussion Questions 89

ACKNOWLEDGEMENTS

As I sit here at my desk, trying to reflect back over my life to my original source of love for the written word, I think of my dad. He was a gentle man that was the truest Christian that I have ever known. He taught me so many things about life that I would later pull from my bag of "wisdom" and use. After his death in 2006, I found my childhood Bible on his nightstand. Looking inside I found notations he had made from years of Saturday morning men's Bible study. Few things mean more to me. I feel comforted in the notes he left behind, a connection of sorts. One thing he told me that I can still hear him saying to me "Many people can go to church and claim to be Christian, but it is how you live your life that is important." He was not a boastful man, he was quiet by nature. You could often hear him whistling as he did work around the house. He was always there to listen whenever you needed an ear. He would only give his advice when it was asked for. His love for his children was amazing. That love hit home to me as we were cleaning out his house. But that is another story. One I do hope to write to honor him.

He encouraged me to write and express myself. He would always agree to fund my love of books. He never turned down my desire to buy a book and read. He could have been an English Professor, but he chose a career in engineering because he thought it would provide for his family better than teaching. So I guess I got my love of reading and writing from him. It is a blessing I don't believe that I will ever be able to repay, but one I hope to honor with this book.

I often imagined when I was in high school of writing a book. I was in my high school's literary club. I imagined myself an acclaimed writer. I decided that if I ever published a book, I would use the names of two grandparents to honor them. I would use Nelson for a grandmother that died many years before I was born. She was a gifted oil painter. Something we had in common was the love of painting. And then I would use the name Hardy after my father's side of the family. My grandfather Hardy was a small man in stature, but he had big hands and a big heart. He had a "New Englander's" sense of humor. Often you could not tell if he was telling you the truth or pulling your leg, except for the twinkle in his eyes. He was an electrician by trade that owned and worked a farm to support his eleven children. It was the stories and adventures of this family of thirteen that I grew up learning to love. My dad would often share stories of his family at the dinner table. It is through osmosis, the seeping in of all those stories that I became who I am. They have been in my blood for a long time. I am a true Yankee, born and bred, but transplanted to a southern town when I was a toddler.

In 2007 I decided to return to college. My employer was offering a program where they would pay you back all classes that you maintained a high grade point average. I had wanted to do this for years, so I jumped at the chance. My attitude was that I would take the classes as long as I could, do the best I could. For this opportunity I thank them.

Enter Jeff Wallace. He was my English professor assigned to our cohort class. I ended up having him for three classes. He was a young man who had boundless energy when talking about a subject he loved. The energy he shared with us ignited a fire deep inside me. He re-awakened my love of English, expressing myself through the written word. I believe that if I had not had him for an instructor, I would not have written this book. He encouraged all of us, and gave me just what I needed to start writing again. Thank you Jeff.

I have a number of friends on Facebook that would read my posts and encourage me to keep writing them. They expressed their pleasure in reading what I wrote. A couple of them suggested I write a book about my critters. I tried to write posts that were enjoyable to read, often seeing the humorous side of things. And for my pleasure, I wrote about the intelligence and human characteristics of my critters. For these friends I want to tell them that they spurred me on to take a vastly different career choice by their encouragement to me. I needed to write this book. Thank you for your belief in me.

PREFACE

It's simple, really. I have been blogging about this story for some time now. I have a number of friends that have enjoyed reading about this adventure and encouraged me to put it in print. I started writing again after many years away, through a process people call Adult Education, or night school. When my youngest child was one year away from graduating college, I decided that if I was ever going back to school, I better get on it! The knowledge was through "hands-on" experience, and what I learned from it through observation.

D*ear God,*

Why have you forsaken me? Why have you allowed my life to become such a miserable excuse for a life? I have begged and pleaded with you to heal me and take away my pain, to give me hope that my life will get better. I have hit rock bottom God. I have lost my friends, my family. I've been shunned from work. Why do you allow such disgrace to be heaped on my shoulders? I don't know what you are trying to teach me God. I have begged for your mercy, yet I have not heard from you. I don't have the strength anymore God. I can't glorify you when I feel like I am bleeding to death. If you think I am such a miserable person, Hell isn't good enough for me. You created each and every living being on this earth. You have the power to make them good. Why do you allow them to stray? Are you bored God? Is having a good and peaceful earth not interesting enough for you? Do you allow us to stray so you can choose who you help, and who you punish? You can change everyone's heart. You can heal them. Why don't you? I'm at the end of my rope God. Are you going to let me fall? Or are you going to give me your hand?

I included this prayer to help you understand where I was prior to writing this book. It was a difficult time for me. I had been through a lot of emotional distress, and that had taken a toll on my health. I questioned God, I was losing faith in Him. I'd lost two parents to a debilitating disease that took away the very center of their being. I'd lived in agony watching them die a slow death, knowing that I couldn't do a single thing to help them. What they had was incurable . Alzheimer's is a terrible way to die. And then my oldest brother died suddenly. I was also watching my marriage fall apart. I realize now that my grief for my parents and brother gave me the strength to face the devastating events surrounding my divorce. It strengthened me in a way that I didn't realize. God was at work, although I didn't see it then.

The years immediately after my divorce were hard. I set up a budget to try to pay all my bills. After reworking my house mortgage to allow me to make lower payments,

I was left with a monthly budget of twenty five dollars for groceries. My hunger caused me to pilfer the garbage can for uneaten food. I worked late most evenings, so I was able to gather the food undetected and place it in my purse. That way I was able to eat in the evenings when I went home. I bought eggs, cereal, powdered milk, and sometimes bread if it was marked down.

It was also a time of grief. I often released my sorrow by crying myself to sleep at night. In the mornings I would smear Preparation H on my eyelids to try to reduce the swollen lids so I could go to work with some semblance of normalcy.

I dealt with two back surgeries by myself. My companions were my three dogs. They loved me and gave me warmth when my furnace went out and the temperature dipped below zero. One of the dogs was an outside dog, and not used to staying in the house. He was gassy that night. Every time he passed gas, he would jump up, turn around and look at me, thinking I was the culprit that let loose with such a putrid odor. That was an experience that I can now laugh at, but it was a struggle to stay warm and tested my survival skills.

I had a car accident at Christmastime that totaled my car and also totaled some of my teeth. I'd just gotten them fixed after a previous injury. Some friends and coworkers asked me the following Monday mornings what happened over the weekend *this* time. It got to be a running joke.

Easter 2009

I sat in church that morning and listened to Steve, my pastor, talk about the Sunday after Easter being anticlimactic. I realized how lucky I was to be there. On Thursday, April 9th my blood sugar climbed so high that it affected Good Friday through Easter Sunday. Thursday afternoon at work I had a headache that just wouldn't quit. I got a new prescription of insulin in the mail and planned on changing out my pump reservoir when I got home. That evening I checked my blood sugar before bed, and found it was extremely high. It was over six hundred, so I made it a point to put in a new port when I changed the reservoir. I noticed that the cannula had crimped and I had not been getting insulin. That was why my blood sugars were so high. Thinking that would take care of things, I retired for the night.

When I woke up on Friday morning, I felt like I was coming down with a stomach virus. I called Annie, my supervisor, and told her I wouldn't be at work on Friday. I started vomiting about 12:30 that afternoon and didn't stop until sometime Sunday. I knew I could get dehydrated, so I tried to drink some water each time

I threw up. The longest it stayed down was ten minutes. My son came by on Saturday to see me. When he saw me, he fixed me something to drink and cleaned out my pan after I spit up into it. He was reluctant to leave, but I told him I would be fine when the virus ran its course. I didn't want to give him whatever I had caught. Monday morning rolled around, and I vaguely remember talking to my manager on the phone. She said something to me about calling Connie, my daughter. I told her that I didn't think Connie would come because she worked in a school two counties away. I don't remember hanging up the phone. I do remember sitting on the john and hearing what sounded like the cavalry coming up my driveway. There was someone knocking on the back door, and I called out to them to wait "just a minute." I made it to Connie's room to look out the window and saw Tom, my son in law, running down to the basement door. I turned to go back into the bathroom to flush the toilet. I knew the basement door was open and Tom could get in that way.

The next half hour was a flurry of movements, bits and pieces jumbled and scattered. A young woman helped me down the hallway and pulled up a chair for me to sit on while she questioned me. "When did I start throwing up? What was yesterday? What was today? Who is the president?" My lips just wouldn't form Obama. They were so dry they were sticking to my teeth. It hurt to think. She called out to Travis, the other EMT, and said she needed to bring me down. Immediately, a young man was in front of me as I tried to negotiate the staircase. Tom grabbed my shoes and purse and I grabbed a two liter bottle of Sprite Zero as I neared the back door.

Magically, as the back door opened, a gurney was on the porch for me to sit on. Amy and Travis put me into the ambulance *sideways* and started telling me what they needed to do. Connie climbed up front with Travis and Tom followed in their car. Amy inserted an IV into my left arm. It infiltrated within moments, so she started one in my right arm. I told her to use a child's IV.

Amy stepped to my head and spoke into some sort of phone. She said I was tachycardia 188, with a blood sugar reading over four hundred. She allowed me a big gulp of Sprite before going up the driveway. I asked her to tell me how she ever got started as an EMT. She had been a music major in college, but she found it to be dull and boring. Those were her words, not mine. It turned out Travis went to school with my son, and Amy's husband graduated with Connie.

As we hit 127, I tried to close my eyes. I have always gotten car sick easily, and I was flying sideways down the road. Definitely, the trees flying past upset my equilibrium. I spent nine and a half hours in the ER on Monday. They transferred me to ICU later that night. After speaking to an internist on the floor that night, he correctly evaluated my need for more fluid and ordered another bag of IV fluid.

The funny thing was I was not frightened during this experience. I felt sort of like I was a spectator instead of the participant in all of it. The next morning when I woke up, I felt differently. I was sore from head to foot. My throat hurt from all the throwing up, and my sides ached from it as well. I had a horrid headache, my hip hurt where the strap from the gurney had been, my inner arms were tender from the IV's, and the electrodes had removed the top layer of skin in twenty six different spots. But I was alive.

Thank you God!

That experience on Easter weekend made me start thinking about two things. I started to question why I continued to work at a place that was so unequal and jeopardized my health so badly. Secondly, I wondered about the voice that I had heard in the emergency room. It was a voice that I have heard on different occasions in my life; a voice that I could not ignore. My Father told me to "Get your house in order." That was enough to shake anyone up. But, it did prepare me for some events that followed not long afterwards.

When I lost my job in the fall of 2010, I believed that I would be able to find another job fairly soon. I had been unemployed once before when a retail store I worked at closed down. I expected to be off work for a matter of months. So when my pastor spoke about different mission trips that we could sign up for, I found myself volunteering to go on one. I don't know why, except that my heart held a great longing to do something that I had always wanted to do but never had the chance. The urge to volunteer was close to a compulsion, something I could not control. Imagine my surprise when I went up to my pastor after the service and told him that I wanted to volunteer, and he said, "Sure, which one do you want to do?" I was so shocked that I felt I was stuttering and blubbering incoherently. I think I got the message across that I would read about the different trips and get back with him. Well, I was committed now.

That one mission trip opened up three more opportunities for me to serve in unexpected ways. I could sew, so I made clothing and provided material for one mission trip to Jamaica and two more to Honduras. I was depleting my store of fabric (in accordance with getting my house in order!) and had a great feeling of accomplishment and peace. The children receiving the clothing had very little, and the school in Jamaica was so thankful that they took pictures modeling the clothing and sent me handwritten thank-you notes. That simple act soothed my aching heart. It made me feel like I was doing something useful while I was unemployed.

I continued to apply for jobs, with no luck. One financial institution was excited to interview me, noticing that I had recently graduated from college. When I walked into the lobby and asked to speak to the man interviewing, I saw a look of shock on his face when he realized my age. I was an adult that had gone back to night school to obtain my degree. One question that he asked me was "Where or what would you like to be doing in five years' time?" I answered that I would like to have written and published a book. He shook my hand at the end, and said he would be looking for my book. I got the rejection message on my telephone at home. Wow. That was unprofessional. Maybe it was a good thing that I had not been offered a job there. I consoled myself that God was working for me to have a *better* job, one that I would be good at. He knew what I needed.

It started in July of 2011. I had been out working on my garden wall, trying to rebuild it after a large colony of chipmunks had made so many tunnels behind the rock that it had caved in. I started at one end, and was about six feet down the wall before realizing what the problem was. I went to a nearby nursery and got a truck bed load of good soil. As I pulled out the fallen rock, taking it to the ground, I tamped soil in the vacant areas where all the tunnels were.

It was slow work; hot, because it was out in the July sun, and sweaty, because it was physically challenging. Some of the rocks were difficult to pick up, move, and set in place because they were heavy. The ones that I couldn't easily pick up I managed to work in place using a heavy iron pry bar to help me. I was very aware of keeping my fingers away when I dropped the rock in place. My Dad had an accident when I was in high school working on a rock wall. Caught his finger between two rocks and smashed it pretty good. And, Dad, being Dad, taped the finger shut with a couple band aids! I didn't want that to happen to me.

I had come in to cool off, drink a large cold drink of tea, and fix some water to take back outside with me. It was late afternoon. My body was telling me I needed to quit for the day. My face was red. I could feel my pulse in my face. As I was sitting, drinking, wiping the sweat off my face, my son came in the back door. I heard him swing the door shut, and come walking down the back hallway in search of me. When he got to the living room doorway, he stopped. I could see that he was upset. His face was pale and his expression was anxious. I asked him if everything was alright. "I need your help, outside."

My first thought was he had been in an accident. I got up out of the chair and set down the drink and washcloth. Stuck my feet back into my shoes and followed him out the back door. When I got outside, I looked around for some major wreckage on his RAV 4. He motioned me to the front of the car, and pointed to the grill. "I hit a bird. It flew up in front of the car." When I started looking at the grill, he told me it was stuck under the radiator. I walked closer and bent down for a better look. Sure enough, I could see two feet flailing around trying to help turn the bird right side up again. It wasn't having much luck. I stood up and told Chase to go in and get me a wire coat hanger. His eyes opened wider, and I could tell he was concerned what I was going to do with it.

When he came back out with the hanger, I took it, twisted it, and gently worked it under the bird. Very carefully, I pulled on the hanger, and worked the bird out from under the radiator. I took one quick look, and my stomach clenched. This bird was hurt badly. I took it inside and asked Chase to go down in the basement and get an empty box. When he came back up, I laid down some paper towels and set the bird in the box. I turned around and looked at Chase. "Honey, this bird is not going to make it. It broke its wing when it hit the grill. And the impact busted its side wide open. It's lost a lot of blood. You can tell looking at its eyes that it is going into shock. The fact that it let me pick it up is another indication it's in bad shape. I don't think it will last through the night."

I hated having to tell him this. I remembered all the times as a child he would bring home an injured animal for me to nurse. They hadn't survived. We had so many shoe boxes buried out in the side woods. I knew this would be the same by tomorrow morning. He looked at me with those sad, puppy dog eyes. "Will you try? Doves are my favorite. Please Mom?" I remembered those words. "P-l-l-l-l-e-a-s-e Mom." How could a child make so many syllables out of a one syllable word! I blinked. My watery eyes saw the young man before me, with his trusting eyes. I couldn't say no.

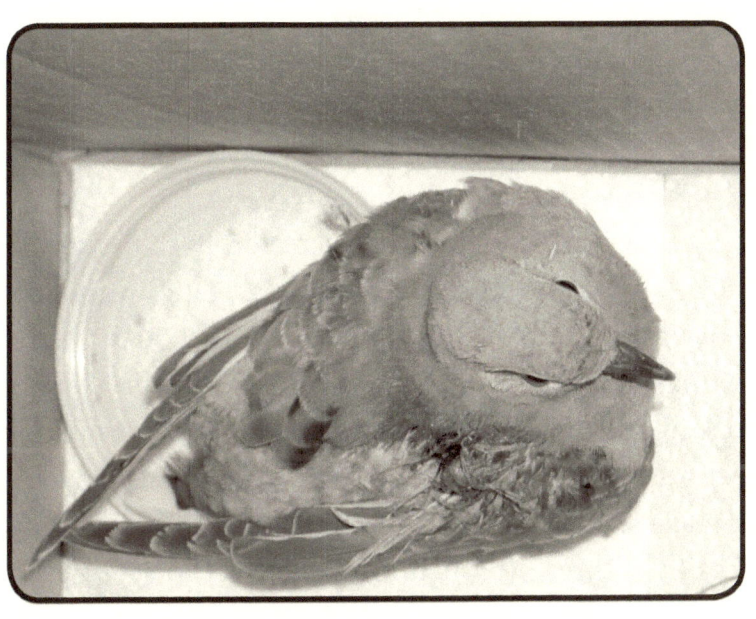

"Okay. We'll use the dining room table. It has the best light. Let me get some things upstairs. I'll be right back." Trying to make a mental list of what I needed, I climbed the stairs. Sewing needle and thread, Betadine wash, hand towel, alcohol for my hands, syringe, and my glasses so I could *see*! I set these down on the table and went to pick up a few more items. A puppy pad, from when I was house breaking Hanna. That would be a clean absorbent surface to put the bird on. I went in the bathroom and washed my hands, and then splashed a liberal amount of alcohol on my hands.

I got a bowl from the cabinet and dropped the needle down in some alcohol too. The thread I put in another bowl that I poured Betadine wash. I let it soak up the orangey brown liquid. I threaded the needle. "Okay, I need you to hold the flashlight right on the spot so I can see to sew her up. You might have to help me hold her." I made short threads so I wouldn't have to pull a long length of thread through her skin. I looked at her eyes. They were weak looking and didn't seem able to focus, which was probably better. I figured I better try and get the side sewn up first. Taking the threaded needle I poked it through a piece of skin and looked for the matching flap on the other side. When I pulled it through and got a good anchor, I reached over and dunked a Q-tip in the Betadine. I let it run all over the wound. I didn't swab it, because I didn't want to introduce any more germs into the wound. Very gently, I proceeded to sew the rest of the wound together. I was careful not to pull too hard or fast. I didn't want the thread to act as a knife and slice through the delicate skin. When I got to the end of the wound I knotted it off. I swabbed some more of the Betadine on for good measure.

Now, for the hard part. Chase helped me open the broken wing so I could see it better. The bone had broken, but there was still a tendon connecting the two pieces of wing. If I could get the bone back together, so it would grow back together, she might have a chance. I reached over and opened a clean, sterile syringe. I used some pliers that I had dipped in alcohol to pull out the steel needle. Very carefully, I eased the end of the needle into one end of the bone.

I then eased the other side of the bone over to work the needle into the other side of the bone. It didn't want to stay together. I tried a couple times, but each time it seemed to be sapping the strength out of the bird. Her eyes were becoming dull. That wasn't a good sign. I stepped back and took stock of the situation. A bird could live without its wing. It would never be able to fly again. But I could take care of it. She was small. Probably only been flying a few weeks from the looks of her. She could fit in one hand. She still had her fledgling spotted feathers.

Okay, let's try another approach. I got a longer piece

of thread and knotted it. Stepped up to the bird, and bent it's wing back and forth so I could find the joint. I proceeded to push the needle through the joint. When it was through, I did the same to the shoulder joint. My thought was I could secure the broken bone until it healed, she might not flap around and injure it more. I set her down in the box. My hands were spotted with blood and iodine wash. I went once again and washed them. As I was washing my hands I thought of an incident that had happened a few months before.

A friend who breeds and raises dogs had one elderly dog that looked like it was going to die. He mixed up a solution of Zija™, and fed it to the dog in small doses over the weekend. The nutrition in the Zija™ helped revive the dog. So, I mused…what could it hurt? I didn't expect the bird to live anyway. So why not give it a try. I got a cup of water and mixed in the Zija™powder. I got a couple clean Q-tips and dunked one into the cup. I nudged the bird's mouth. It eagerly sucked on the Q-tip and swallowed the fluid. I picked her back up and fed her this way until she would not take any more fluid. I looked at her, still so weak.

Okay God. I've done all I can for this little bird. The rest is up to you. You heard what Chase said. It's his favorite. God, I know it's your will, but we could really use some visible sign that you're with us here. We've had some difficult times, and I really don't want to dig another grave tomorrow. Please God; heal this little bird, for your Glory.

I set the little bird back in the box. She crouched down in the bottom of the box. I had put a robin's nest in the box, just in case she wanted some place to snuggle up. It might look comforting to have something from nature in the box with her.

Chase came back in the house from putting his flashlight back in the car. I told him we had done all we could. I asked him to say a special prayer for Glory. "Glory? Where did you get that name?" "Oh, I don't know. I thought it was appropriate." Chase took the box up and set it on his dresser. He worked night shift, so he went on to bed when he got up there.

The next morning I gently opened the bedroom door. I hesitated, not wanting to go in and find yet another little animal that had not made it. I stuck my head in and squinted to see in the darkened room. It was quiet. I didn't want to wake up my son. But as my eyes adjusted to the dim light, I could see a shape over by the box. I tiptoed closer... as I got within a few feet, there was a little head looking around the room. It was doing the same thing I was doing, peering around the room, trying to see where it was. I leaned close enough to look down into the box. I didn't know how the bird could be peeking over the box edge when last night it could barely stand up.

Okay, that's it! The bird was balanced on the edge of the nest I had put in the box for comfort. In fact, its feet were grabbing hold and wiggling a little trying to steady itself. It turned its head and looked at me curiously. I eased my hands around the box, and tiptoed back out the door. I carried it all the way downstairs to the dining room before stopping. When I set the box down, she cocked her head sideways and looked at me. I felt like she was taking my measure, checking me out.

Well I'll be. It worked. Thank you God!

I made a couple little chirping noises to try and reassure her. I walked swiftly over to the kitchen counter looking for the packet of Zija™ powder. Mixing it into cold water, I grabbed some Q-tips and went back to the box. Once again, I hand fed the bird with a Q-tip. I fed her until she would take no more. When I was done, she shook the water droplets off her beak and proceeded to preen her feathers. She gingerly worked around her injured side and wing. I had looked on the internet to see what doves ate. There were a few things I had in the kitchen to make do until I could get to town to purchase some real bird food.

I gathered the stuff from the pantry. I mixed them together and placed the food in a canning lid. I knew that doves were ground feeders. I wanted the food to be on the floor of the box so she could eat it easily. I mixed some cornmeal, oats, flax seed, and a small amount of poppy seeds. I thought the poppy seeds might work as a pain reliever. She loved the flax seeds. The oatmeal was

too big, so I filtered it back out and chopped them up.
She pecked around in the mixture, actually eating some
of it. She stuck her beak down and pecked around the
mix, lifting her head and making a smacking noise like
she enjoyed the taste. I fed her Zija™ mixed in water and
the muesli mix the rest of the weekend.

She was still awkward and skittish when I tried to pick
her up. I could tell that she didn't trust me holding her. I
tried to avoid touching her injured wing, and cradled her
into my palm. As long as I was feeding her, she sat still. As
soon as I finished, she made a beeline to get back down.
My dog Hanna, was curious about what I was holding. She
would catch a whiff of the bird, and readjust her lips, trying
to catch the drool that was forming in her mouth. I could
read her face very well. It said: tasty snack! I would have to
keep them apart unless I was there to guard the bird.

I could tell Glory was improving each day. She had
more energy, the spark was back in her eyes, and she was
eating greedily. She was jumping up onto the bird's nest
edge frequently, trying to escape. I knew a trip to the pet
store was in the near future. I needed peace of mind that
she was safe, and not in danger of falling into the mouth
of my waiting German Shepherd (GSD). When I went for
bird supplies, I would have to get Hanna a special beef
bone too.

I went into town and went to the new pet store that had opened just a few months before. I found a big beef bone for Hanna. And I found a bird cage that would work for the bird's recovery period. It had a couple perches that she could hold on to, and two different feeders. One I used for her water, the other for her seed. I got an idea that if I could put a level spot in the cage off the floor, she could use that as her nesting platform. I needed to get something that was easy to wash off, and non-porous so it wouldn't hold bacteria.

I went to Lowe's and purchased a tile that you would use to tile a bathroom. Then I got a piece of half inch caging and bent it around the perch. On top of that I placed the tile. Glory was eyeing me suspiciously, watching every move I made. When I finished it, I picked up Glory and gently placed her on the tile. There was a slight incline to the tile. Glory tensed up. You could see she didn't like the slick surface of the tile. And she slid off! The tile prevented her from getting a good hold on the platform.

Once down, she wouldn't get back on it. I tried placing her back on the tile a few more times. I took the tile out, considering what to do. Glory walked to within a few paces of the caging. She cocked her head and looked at it at an angle. And then she ever so easily jumped up on the wire caging! She walked around as if testing it out, and nestled down on the platform. That would solve another problem I had. I no longer had to clean off the tile from her droppings. They fell right through. And it seemed like she liked being able to look through the wire caging. The see through fencing made the cage appear bigger too.

I started blogging about Glory on my website. I wanted to share with my friends the story of this amazing little bird, and her spunk and determination to get better. Watching her fight to get better gave me renewed hope about my job situation. It gave me something to do which I have always loved; nurturing. Watching something grow and thrive. I didn't know it at the time, but the good Lord was giving me something to occupy my time while I waited for His will to be done in my life. It was a low time in my life, but not the lowest. I frequently wrote to God, my feelings of inadequacy written down so I could look back on my progress, and remember where I had been.

July 10, 2011

I took Glory out in the front yard today. She looked up at me for a few moments when I sat her down on the ground. Then she started pecking at little bugs and seeds on the ground. I figured she was full when she squatted down and closed her eyes. A full belly makes me sleepy too.

July 11, 2011

When I went in to check on Glory this morning, she popped her head up and cocked her head sideways to look at me as I approached. I knew she hadn't grown six inches overnight. When I got close enough to look inside the box, she was standing on the edge of the bird nest, her toes gripping tightly to the side. So tightly, she was shaking the nest and her knees were knocking. She looked like me on roller skates!

July 14, 2011

This morning when I brought Glory down to clean out her box and feed her, I turned my back for just a moment. I heard a noise, turned around, and she was perched on top of the box! She had jumped (or flown) over a foot, straight up to reach the top of her box. I'm leaving the house now to get a birdcage.

July 15, 2011

I think Glory likes her new house. She can see everything going on in the room. I caught her preening this morning and pulling at her stitches.

July 17, 2011

Something incredible happened this morning! I got Glory out of her cage. She flapped her wings quite a bit. As she raised her wings I saw something on her injured wing that I hadn't seen before. I gently spread her wing and saw what looked like rows of claws. I think she is growing new feathers where she lost them. I've never had a bird before, so I'll have to keep you posted. I've continued to feed her Zija™.

July 19, 2011

I was sitting at my sewing machine yesterday when Hanna did something very touching...she came up to me and laid her hedgehog in my lap. When she laid it down, she whined and looked up at me. Upon investigation, the stuffed animal had its stuffing coming out, and its squeaker was broken. I wonder if she remembers me sewing up Glory?

July 20, 2011

A neat thing happened this morning with Glory. When I took the cover off her cage, she was very sleepy. When I stuck my hand in there for her to climb on my finger, she took her wing and hit me. It was like she was showing me she wasn't awake yet, and was pushing me back, just like a human child would do. She's a spunky little thing.

July 21, 2011

Glory spent a lot of time preening yesterday. This morning it looks like she has a bunch of cowlicks sticking up at odd angles. The quills have little tufts of feather sticking out of them.

July 22, 2011

When I took Glory's cover off her cage this morning, she actually spoke to me! She must have been hungry, because she started whisper chirping to me when she saw me replacing the bird seed. I checked her feathers today. The feathers have grown out a half inch. And she has tail feathers coming in too!

July 23, 2011

I thought I had found the perfect place for Glory's cage. I hung her in my computer space at the top of the stairs. I'm sitting here with flax seed raining down...

maybe it wasn't such a good place after all. Every time she does it, she looks down and checks my reaction!

July 24, 2011

I just got home from the grocery with a new bag of bird feed. As I turned around from dumping her old food, she had both wings up and she was pumping for all she was worth! She looked magnificent! She's now chowing down on the new stuff and chirping her approval.

July 26, 2011

Glory is working harder each day to strengthen her wings. I might have to get her a bigger cage. She likes me whistling to her, and will come to the side of the cage and look down at me. She also likes spraying me with seeds. I wonder what head bobbing means in dove talk?

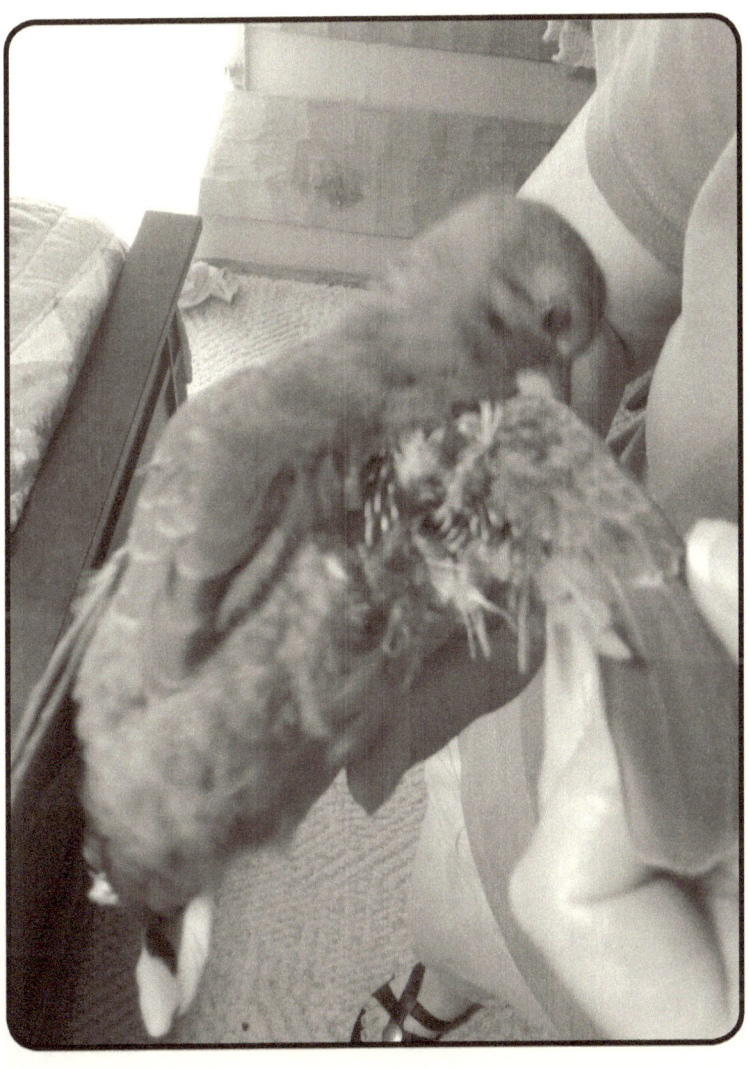

July 27, 2011

An old man once said, "There comes a time in your life when you walk away from all the drama and people who create it. You surround yourself with people who make you laugh. Forget the bad, focus on the good. LOVE the people who treat you right, pray for the ones who don't. Falling down is part of life. Getting back up is living." Glory is teaching me to get back up!

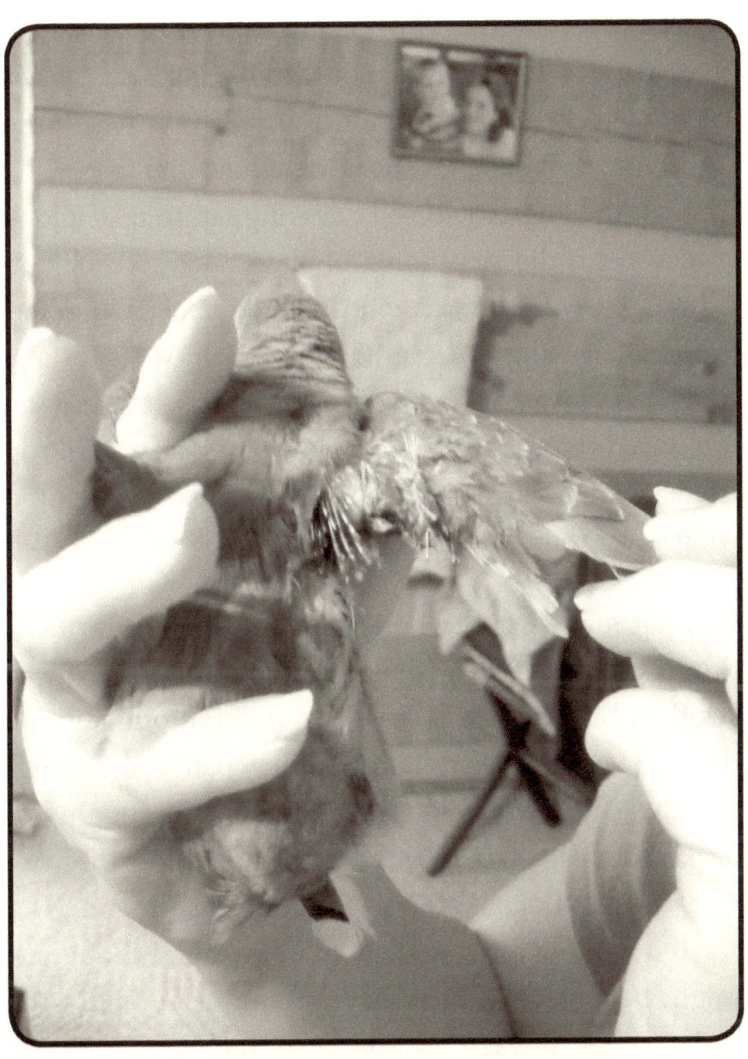

August 1, 2011

Okay everybody... I'm shaking so badly that I don't know if I can type this or not. I took Glory out of her cage to check on her progress. I usually take her in the bathroom, so if she flies she is contained and doesn't fly through the house. I spread her wing out to take a look at it. When I did that, something dropped to the floor. I didn't see what it was, but looking at her wing, her feathers have almost covered up the bald spot. In fact, when she's just standing there, you can't see where she was hurt. (There is still a small piece of thread sticking up from her stiches) Except for the fact she holds her injured wing lower than the other one.

I felt for the spot where the bone sticks out of the skin. I didn't feel it. I turned her over, her elbow was swollen, but there was no bone sticking out. By this time, my hands were shaking pretty badly, and Glory was shaking because she was frightened. I brought her back to her cage and placed her on her platform. Then I went back to the bathroom, got down on all fours, and started looking for what had fallen off her. I thought it might be a piece of bird seed. I found it up under the sink cabinet. It was about 3/8 of an inch long. I picked it up...

It was the piece of wing bone that she had broken

when she hit the car. I can't find where it had stuck out of her skin.

Thank you God!

August 3, 2011

Glory's quiet this morning. I guess with it being overcast she thinks it's still night time! She's making little chirps, sort of like she's singing to herself.

I took Glory out to make progress pictures this afternoon. She was on my shoulder and we wanted to see if she would transfer to my son's shoulder. Instead she climbed up on my head! It felt really funny to feel her toes grabbing hold of my hair!

August 5, 2011

I put Glory on my shoulder last night while I was sitting at the computer. She was quiet and still for a long time. I looked around and she was looking in my ear... Chase thought she was looking for bird seed. Ha ha, Chase.

August 7, 2011

Saturday I went to the library and checked out a cd on songbirds. When I put it in this morning, Glory got up on her perch and was very quiet. When it played the dove section, she jumped down and ran around her cage and looked down and all around for the other dove. I was hoping she would call out to the other dove...

August 10, 2011

I snipped the stitches loose on Glory this morning. I took her in my bedroom to test out her flying ability. She can fly, but it looks a little forced, not smooth yet. I did catch her stretching that wing, balancing on one leg. She was stretching the leg under her injured wing while balancing on her left leg. Hmm, is that yoga?

August 12, 2011

I took Glory out in the front yard today to see how far she could fly. She flew about seventy five feet. When I found her she was winded and panting. I put her on a cherry tree branch until she calmed down and got her wind. I walked over and stood close to the branch. Glory hopped onto my shoulder.

August 17, 2011

Boy, did I get a scare this morning! When I walked out into the hallway heading for the bathroom, there was a flurry of wings and feathers over by my computer. Hanna was over there in a flash. I could see fricasseed dove for her breakfast. When I told her no, she backed away and looked at me. When I called Glory, she walked out from under the chair and headed over to me. I don't know how she got the cage door open...but I did remember that Glory had made a light ruckus last night after I had gone to bed. I was almost asleep and I heard her hitting her wings against the cage. After just a few minutes, she quieted down. I thought she had gone to sleep. By that time she was probably already out of her cage and on the floor. It was probably a long night for her. There were several places that she could hide for the night, but I still felt bad that she was frightened and had to hide.

August 24, 2011

I think Glory is checking out my new haircut. You know how beauticians will "play" with your hair as they cut it to make sure there are no long straggles? Well, she's back there pulling on the bottom hairs on my neck. I think she's grooming me!

August 29, 2011

This morning Glory was sitting in my lap while I was at the computer. Hanna came up beside me and smelled Glory. Now, Hanna has a big nose, and she's very curious. She accidently goosed the bird; the bird took off, scrambled up my sleeve, and dropped a bomb on Hanna's nose. It happened so fast, Hanna didn't know what hit her.

September 6, 2011

I found a really neat cd at Bass Pro Shop yesterday. It has the sounds of nature around a lake. Crickets, birds, water lapping on the shore, and a loon off on the lake somewhere. Sooo peaceful. I'll enjoy listening to it this winter when everything is silent. (Glory likes it too!)

September 7, 2011

Glory did something amazing this afternoon! She had been perched on my shoulder for a while...she kept looking up at her cage above me and cocking her head. All at once, she jumped off my shoulder, did an upwards spiral around my head and landed on her cage door. Then she just hopped into the cage and up onto her seed feeder. I guess she was hungry.

September 8, 2011

Glory and I have been cold the last two days...I'm wearing leggings and a big fleece sweater with a knitted cowl neckline. Glory likes to climb into the back of the neckline and nestle in like she has a soft nest. Glory's all fluffed up holding air in her feathers to stay warm. She looks twice her size. Hanna's lovin' it!

September 9, 2011

Glory is on my shoulder trembling. Her whole body is shaking. I cradled her in my hand, and slowly blew a hot breath on her. She cocked her head to look up at me, and then nestled against my arm. I guess that helped to warm her up...

September 10, 2011

You know you have a well-trained dog when she will put her nose on a bird, and then back off when you tell her to. I told Hanna that Glory is Mama's bird, just like Hanna is Mama's dog. Hanna didn't look too happy with that news.

September 13, 2011

Glory has started doing something different. She gets up next to my ear or neck, and then she shivers…it's sort of like a cross between a hummingbird's wing sound, and a cat purring. Not sure what it means…

Glory found a stitch that I had missed on her wing. She plucked and pulled until it was quite long. I took some cuticle scissors and snipped it off. Her wings have filled in nicely. Her tail feathers are slow in coming in. They look a little ragged.

Glory will now willingly hop on my hand when I stick it in her cage. She even knows to *duck* her head when I pull my hand back out of the cage. We are learning new things every day!

September 18, 2011

Philippians 2:13 (Christian Standard Bible) …God "works in you" to will and to act according to His good purpose. This passage really hit home for me tonight. It's one I can relate to in my own life. We, as humans do not understand all the passages of the Bible, but certain verses will touch our heart like no others.

September 23, 2011

Hanna just wedged Mr.Bunny in the bedroom door so my son couldn't close the door on her. Glory "whoos" me every time I answer her. She'll keep it up until I change to a chirping sound, cock her head to get a better look, and then starts repeating the sounds I make. Ah, family life!

September 28, 2011

I changed Glory's water this morning. I just watched her drink her fill. Then she proceeded to jump *in* the water dish and cool her feet off. If you could just see the expression on her face as she stood there in the cold water. Priceless!

October 13, 2011

Yesterday morning, I took Glory outside with me while I picked up the sticks that fell when I cut down that tree in the front yard. I put her in the barrel of the wheel barrow. She immediately scampered up on the edge of the barrow so she could see where we were going. She stood on my shoulder as I bent and picked up sticks. Each time I bent over, I could feel her toenails tighten so she wouldn't fall off. When I got within 12 feet of the woods, she took flight when I bent down once again. She landed in a honeysuckle bush on the edge of the woods. As I approached her, I could see she was wedged in between three branches. Her flight caused a blue jay to notice her. It flew closer, angrily squawking and swooping. This frightened her and she took off again, heading for the creek. I didn't see where she landed because of the slight hill beside the creek edge.

I had to walk around some obstacles to get to the general area where she had flown. I wasn't worried because I could usually find her within a few minutes. But this time when I got to where I *thought* she had landed, she wasn't there. The ground by the creek was covered in dried leaves, Sycamore bark, and dead grass. All this made an ideal cover and hiding place for a bird that was marked just like the ground. She blended right into the ground cover. A couple times I bent down thinking I had found her when I realized that it was a piece of bark.

Slowly, I walked up and down where I thought she had landed. Every few feet, I stopped and stood very still. If she moved, I *thought* I could hear her walking through the crisp leaves.

My eyes started stinging with the tears I was forcing back. When my eyes started burning, I blamed it on the smoke from the fire. I had one last chance. I could go get Hanna and bring her outside to help me find Glory. But I hesitated, knowing that some predator could come along in an instant and she would surely be gone for good. There was pressure in my chest. My eyes were freely running. I didn't bother to wipe them. In a moment of deep sadness, I started wailing in dove talk. I was letting out all my grief in the saddest "coo" I could wail. I wasn't ready to say goodbye to my little Glory.

I opened my eyes and blinked rapidly to squeeze the tears that were overflowing. My eyes scanned the creek one last time. How could I explain my carelessness to my son? The corner of my eye detected movement on down the creek. It was just a quick, smooth, ever so silent move. If I had had my eyes closed, I would have missed it. I blinked again to focus on something thirty feet away. I jumped into the creek, scraped my head on a branch, and started running as fast as the uneven ground would allow me towards that movement. Glory was standing in the middle of the creek bed, with her head cocked sideways, looking at me as if to say "What on *Earth* was that mournful noise?"

When I was within fifteen feet of her, she turned around and resumed her meanderings down the dry creek bed. She was walking from side to side, looking under leaves, checking out hidey-holes, and pecking at bugs near rocks. She wasn't worried in the least. She could see me. I knew I had to pick her up soon. If she went in the culverts, there was no way I would go in after her. Spiders lived in the culverts. Ugghhh! As I bent down to pick her up, she crouched to jump in my outstretched hand. She had a few feathers on her wings that were bent cock-eyed. I knew she had had another crash landing. I held her close to my chest, using both hands to cradle her close to me. She hunkered up close to me, looking at me sideways as I scrambled up the creek bank and headed towards the house. I explained to her that even though she had fun, I had work to do. My hands were still trembling when I got to the house.

October 15, 2011

Last night Glory was on my shoulder. A ladybug flew down by my computer. I picked it up and put it on my shoulder to see what Glory would do with it. She walked over, cocked her head to get a better look, pecked at it a couple times, and then she sat on it! When Glory got up and moved to my other shoulder, the lady bug stood up and hurriedly walked away!

November 21, 2011

For the past few months I have enjoyed taking care of an injured bird that was hit by a car. I have learned what types of food she likes and dislikes, her innate curiosity, her way of looking at the world (with her head cocked to one side), and that patience worked when she was learning to trust the person that sewed her back together without first administering pain killer. But this past Friday I learned something new about her that ended up making me laugh at myself.

I had an appointment in Lexington after lunch, so I rummaged through the fridge looking for something to eat while I fixed my hair. I grabbed a bag of veggies that would be easy to pop in my mouth while I used my hands to get ready. I had fixed Brussels sprouts the night before and had put the leftovers in a Ziploc bag. They were a perfect finger food. No mess, no fuss. When I was ready I left for Lexington and ended up being gone for several hours.

Climbing the stairs to my computer, I heard Glory jump down off her perch and start cooing to me. Since I hadn't checked my emails that day, I took Glory out of her house as I sat down. She climbed up my arm and settled on my right shoulder. When I started typing she would make little chipping sounds. It's a little noise she makes when she is content. You can also tell when she is falling asleep, because the chips get softer and further apart in duration.

Unfortunately, the veggies I ate for lunch have an unusual effect on me. To put it bluntly, they give me gas. As I was typing away, with a dozing bird on my shoulder, I accidently passed gas. Within seconds I realized it was a killer! And a few seconds after that, Glory was up and on the move. She padded around my neck, over to my left shoulder. She was looking around, looking down towards the floor. I could feel her claws dig into my sweater and scrape my skin as she leaned over and once again surveyed the floor. I quickly glanced over at her, and the expression on her face was one of accusation and shock. Her eyes were open wide, and she was cocking her head to get a better look at me. Looking me up and down. With that expression, I expected her to start shaking her head, and hear tisking noises coming out of her beak. I didn't have to have her say anything to know she had figured out where the noxious fumes had come from. Her beady little eyes were wide open and staring right at me!

Then she started looking up at her cage and judging

the distance from my shoulder to her door. Boy was I feeling guilty. I stood up and walked over to her cage. I ran my fingers through her belly and lifted up. That usually makes her jump up on my hand. She didn't waste any time jumping into her house. I closed the door, bent over and pulled her cover over her cage to try and block the smell from her house. I sat back down, thinking about what had just happened. Then I started laughing. Glory can smell, and has reasoning powers strong enough to make me feel guilty. What will I learn next?

November 24, 2011

I had a wonderful Thanksgiving with new friends to blend in with family. Everyone wanted to meet Glory. My grandchildren helped me make Christmas wreaths to take to the nursing home in town. Hanna got a monster shank bone to celebrate the holiday. I put Glory upstairs so she wouldn't be stressed smelling the turkey roasting!

November 26, 2011

Glory has been losing feathers on her back and head. The new feathers are growing in now. She looks like she has a new SPIKED hairdo! Went to Jefferson Street Mission this morning and served over one hundred and twenty people chili and sandwiches. We received many compliments to the chefs for the three bean chili. We had none left! Good group of friends to work with. I extended my Thanksgiving into the weekend.

November 27, 2011

One of the cute things I have observed Glory doing is raising her wings, looking like she is going to take flight. But instead she raises her wings up high, and then proceeds to stretch one of her legs out directly underneath the wing. It reminds me of a Yoga move that Tony Horton might do on one of his exercise videos. She will usually stretch both her legs before nestling back down on my shoulder and snoozing.

December 1, 2011

I mixed up a batch of groats, wheat germ, and oats for Glory this morning. The oats were a little big, so I had to crumble them up into small bits so she could eat them. I sprinkled a pinch on my shoulder, when she wants more she just says... "whoo." I ran into Walmart tonight and walked through the department where they put all the markdowns. There was a plastic bag with five dove decoys...I laughed as I wondered what Glory would think of a plastic bird twice her size?!!!

December 5, 2011

I put Glory on Hanna's back this morning. I'm teaching Hanna you do not eat "*friends.*" Anyway, Glory likes the feel of Hanna's soft hair, but Hanna's not so sure. Glory's feet feel like a cat kneading your back, Hanna went around in circles trying to see the bird. Glory looked like she was riding a skateboard. She was quite good actually! Just jump in and HANG ON!!!

December 7, 2011

Glory was watching me eat an apple this morning. I bit off a chunk and offered it to her. She cocked her head, leaned down and pecked at it, stood up and swallowed the juice that was on her beak, and then leaned down again and started breaking off little pieces of apple. Apparently, she likes apple. I wouldn't have guessed it...

December 9, 2011

I put Glory in the bathroom so I could clean out her house. When I went back in there, I had to look for her. She was on the floor, walking between the pocket door and the other part of the bathroom. She reminded me of John Travolta in *Saturday Night Fever,* strutting down the walk, bobbing his head to the music. I saw that and the music popped into my head. She's almost asleep now, so I better put her up before she falls off my shoulder.

February 28, 2012

I have learned something new about Glory! She was on my shoulder this morning and I was talking to her. She walked over to my left ear and put her beak right up next to it and started cooing and chipping in my ear! She knows what my ear is for! It really tickled me.

March 11, 2012

Surround yourself with people who know your worth.

You don't need too many people to be happy,

Just a few real ones who appreciate you for

exactly who you are.

I saw this and posted it on my webpage. I couldn't help wondering if that included Hanna and Glory. I believe that God gave me these two incredible animals to give me a job while I was waiting, to keep me occupied and fulfilled. You can't drown in despair when you have someone that needs you to take care of them.

I have learned so much from Glory. She learned to trust a human after she was injured. That is a miracle in itself. Wild animals do not do well in captivity. They learn very early to stay away from humans. She could no longer fly well enough for me to release her back into the woods. She does not have enough strength or maneuverability in her right wing to live outside. She usually crash lands. She isn't strong enough to fly long distances. So, she learned to adapt, and learned to trust again. Wow. I could learn from her.

March 13, 2012

Today was warm enough to open the window and let Glory sit in the sun. She loved it! Hanna, on the other hand, went outside and dug in the soft mud. Hanna gets a bath tonight!

March 14, 2012

This afternoon, I put a towel down, scattered some seed on it, and put Glory on the towel. I watched her pick out the seed she liked best (cracked corn). When she ate her fill, she walked over to investigate what I was reading in a magazine. She hopped on my lap, walked over to the magazine and started pecking at the page. Then she looked over at me as if to say, "What's going on?" The picture was an ad of whole wheat soda crackers, with flax seeds on top of the cracker. Those are another favorite seed. She was trying to get the seeds off the magazine picture. When she couldn't eat them, she walked back over to my side, put her feet out, and slid down my side like she was on a slide, back to her seeds on the towel.

March 15, 2012

Last night when I got Glory out of her house to spend

some "us" time together, I put her on my stomach so she could walk around. She sauntered down to my knees, looking over the edge of the bed as she walked. As most intelligent people do when they are in a prone position with their eyes semi-closed, I drifted off. I was aware of her making her way up my other leg. The next thing I knew, I didn't feel her walking on me. My eyes sprang open, only to come eyeball to eyeball with her. She had settled near my neck and was napping also!

March 16, 2012

I'm happy to report that Glory is feeling better. She flew into a glass window on Tuesday. I didn't know if she would get better. She looked like the Leaning Tower of Pizza for a few days! That's one thing that Glory doesn't understand. She can see through the glass, so why can't she go through the window?

March 22, 2012

I'm preparing to spend another afternoon in the basement. The last three days we've had tornadoes moving through Kentucky. I've had three friends call and check up on me. God's given me wonderful friends. Hanna saw me bring the laptop down and do the emergency hook up for the basement. I'm sure she remembered that from the day before. She whined to go out. When she came back in, she went immediately to the basement. Smart pup! Tornadoes in Kentucky!

March 23, 2012

Okay, everybody! Check in time. Is everyone all right? I have some downed trees, and my truck has hail damage. While I was sitting in the basement on the landing, Glory was on my shoulder. She was very quiet, not making any noise, but her knees were knocking! She got as close as she could to my neck, but she was still shaking. Hanna stayed at my feet, just lying beside me. Isn't it amazing how animals can sense bad weather? I had a friend email me all through the storm. It really helped to feel connected to someone and not feel abandoned. The good Lord sent a friend to calm my fears in such an amazing way. Thanks Mike!

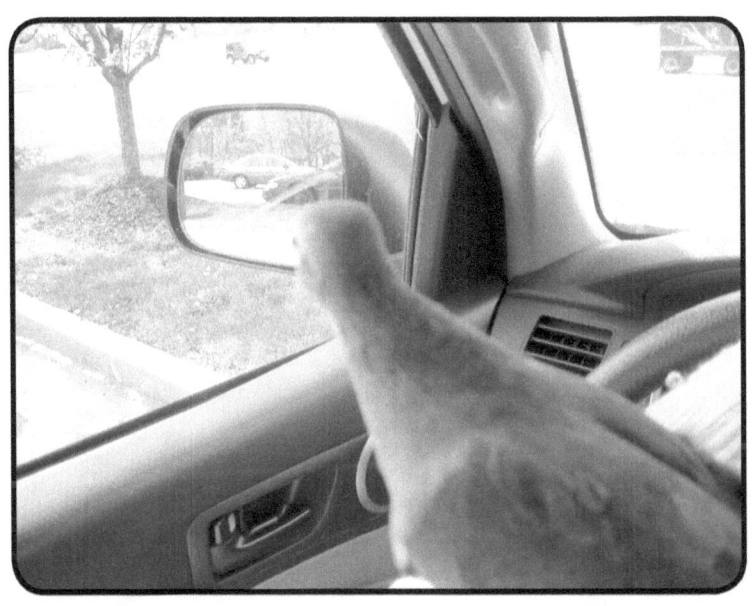

March 24, 2012

Today I drove to Shelbyville to meet Chase. He is going to take care of Glory while I go on a mission trip. I can't believe a year has gone by already. I packed up Glory's food, her cage cover (her blankey), and her cage in the truck. I put her up front in the seat beside me. I thought if she could see me she would be okay. As I was driving up the driveway, I went over a bump and jostled her water dish. It splashed out and ran over the floor of her cage. Glory started flapping around, hitting the door with her wings.

When I got to the top of the hill, I stopped and tried to calm her. She was standing with her wings up and extended, and she was hyperventilating. She kept looking down at the mess on the floor of her cage. I opened the door and stuck my hand in her house. She immediately jumped on my hand and marched herself up my arm until she got to my shoulder. Then she proceeded to stick her beak in my ear and tell me what she thought of my carelessness!

I released the brake and eased onto the pavement while she was on my shoulder. As objects started moving along, they caught her attention and she moved to my left shoulder, closest to the driver's window. She settled down and sat on my shoulder for the rest of the ride. I figured she would be all right as long as I didn't open a window. We stopped at a traffic light. Boy did I get some funny looks!

We got to Shelbyville without any more mishaps, and I pulled into a parking place where we had arranged to meet Chase. Glory was still on my shoulder, but she saw a pair of robins on the ground by a tree, and she walked down my shoulder and along my arm to get a better look. My outside mirror was in her way, so she bent her neck to one side so she could keep track of the robins. They were gathering mulch from a nearby tree and making a nest with it in a tree farther away. Glory watched them for some time. I couldn't help but wonder if she felt the urge to nest and look for a mate. A couple times she looked around at me. Maybe she was checking to see my reaction, I don't know.

A few minutes later Chase pulled up beside my truck and got out. He looked in the truck at the cage. He didn't see Glory, so he asked me where she was. I pointed to my shoulder. He smiled and walked around to the driver's door. When he saw Glory, he started talking to her. She cocked her head to one side and looked up at him. I picked her up by running my fingers under her belly and between her legs. This makes her lift her feet and climb onto my hand. I placed her back in her house. When I opened the door I explained to him about our accident with the water. I suggested we take the wet papers out of the bottom of her cage, and put her cover over her cage so she would be calm while riding to his apartment. I transferred all her gear to his car. We talked a few more minutes about the upcoming week. I gave him a goodbye hug, and got back in the truck. I headed home, he turned towards Louisville. On the way home, something was missing. I realized that I missed my sidekick in the seat next to me. Funny how attached you can get...

March 31, to April 8, 2012

This week was an awesome week. I was once again able to fly to Arizona and help my church help a new church minister to the people in the neighborhoods near Phoenix. I gained so much knowledge and peace from the previous year, that I felt that I could only learn more this year. We did a number of different activities throughout the week. We worked at a food bank, we gave away gift cards from Starbuck's, and we canvassed a neighborhood putting flyers on the doors inviting the neighborhood to attend church services for the following Easter Sunday. We set up tables in a nearby park and served hot dogs and had crafts for the children. We also had a Big Blue party the Saturday we flew in, and again on Monday to watch U of K play. We were able to go hiking at a nearby state park, and also visit Scottsdale and do some "touristy" shopping before we went home. Hanna and Glory were never far from my thoughts. I did notice that there were doves in abundance out there. And if I moved to Arizona, Glory would find many friends.

But the event that broke my heart, and humbled me, was the day that we drove into Phoenix, and distributed water, snack crackers, and socks to people that were living on the streets. It was the first week in April, but the temperatures were hot, and the pavement was scorching. It shocked me that people were laying down on the hot pavement sleeping. They had nowhere else to go.

I had a big trash bag full of assorted socks that I was giving out. All I had to do was hold up a pair in my hand, and people appeared. Many people would ask me if I had a certain kind for their child, or wife. I would dig down in the bag looking for what they needed. Everyone that I encountered was polite to me. They were thankful for what we gave them. Many times their parting comment was "Bless you". It was all I could do not to tear up when I heard those words. Sitting on the bus, riding to the next stop, I had plenty to think about.

Before I left Kentucky, I had been worrying about my job situation and my future. What I learned that week was that I would be taken care of and a peace came over me that I had not experienced in quite a while. I thought about the verse in Matthew and ended up looking it up in my Bible when I got back to my room. It is Matthew 6: 25-34 (Christian Standard Bible).

April 21, 2012

Today, Hanna and Glory had a visitor. Sarah Walker came to the house and wanted to meet Glory. I took her up to Glory's room. Glory looked her over with her head cocked to one side, and proceeded to climb on her hand. She was clucking and chirping her satisfaction. She made a new friend! Hanna enjoyed her visit too. By the end of the visit they had played with the hedgehog, Kong, Frisbee, and various other toys. Both critters were happy. Come back soon Sarah!

April 24, 2012

My new profile picture is when I took Glory for a ride in my truck. She preferred to be on my shoulder, looking out the window instead of her house. She did enjoy watching some robins picking up mulch for a nest while we were waiting for Chase. But it made me wonder if she missed finding a mate to share her life with. Do birds have feelings of longing to have a family?

April 26, 2012,

Tonight I went with a friend to Louisville to attend Joyce Meyer's seminar. I've read a number of her books, and watched several of her dvds, but I've never had the chance to listen to her in person. We sat up towards the top of the arena. It was packed! They had two big screens hanging from the ceiling that had the cameras shooting from different angles. Because they were so big, the audience could see what was going on and got a good view of the stage. The music was great. It was like attending a rock concert with flashing lights and the words to the songs displayed on the screens.

The reason I like her so much is that she talks simply. She explains her message where anyone can understand what she is trying to teach, and she speaks as if she has had firsthand knowledge or experience of what she teaches. She doesn't have a holier-than-thou attitude that many evangelists adopt, and it makes you feel like you are listening to a friend. I have learned a lot in the past, and tonight I learned more.

When the program was over, Frank and I went out in the lobby where she had her DVD's, books, and other souvenirs for sale. We walked around the lobby, finally coming to the end of the tables, where I saw the book I wanted to purchase. It was about forgiveness. I knew that I needed to read this. I felt that it was a subject that would touch my heart. She had some difficult years, and if she could learn to forgive, and wrote about it, it would help me immensely. Try as I might, I still held onto some old grief and baggage that really weighed me down at times. It turned out that the book I bought did help me see things in a different way. I read several of the chapters over and over, and was finally able to let go.

I feel so thankful that I had a friend that invited me to that seminar. Thanks so much Frank. You don't know how much I needed that!

April 30, 2012

It's thundering at my house. I went in Glory's room to check on her. Every time it thundered, she shivered so badly it shook her perch and rattled her cage. It sounded like a phone on silent mode.

May 2, 2012

Last night I went out on the back porch to load up the garbage can into the truck to take to the top of the hill. I heard one lone spring peeper in his pond (Hanna's wading pool) singing out into the night. I smiled, and trilled a response to him. There was an immediate response! I trilled again. He answered me, a little louder this time. I trilled again... This time, he sang for all he was worth. I wondered what he would think of his Lady Love if he could see her on the other side of the forsythia bushes...I stepped off the porch and looked up at the window above me. Glory was in the window, walking back and forth on the sill, looking down at me. I guess she didn't know I was multi-lingual!

May 17, 2012

Hanna and Glory seem to have developed a game they play together. It's sort of like Hide 'n Seek, and Tag, You're it! Glory will sit on the ironing board close to the edge. Hanna will stick her nose up looking for Glory's location. Glory will move to another spot. Hanna cheats and stands up on her back legs to get a peek at Glory. If Glory gets too close to the edge of the board, Hanna will goose Glory! When I told Hanna the other day that Glory bites, Hanna backed away!

May 21, 2012

Yesterday I went out in the yard to pick up sticks. It was such a beautiful day I took Glory out with me. I figured she could walk around in the grass and explore while I was working. I normally put her in a tree while I am outside. In the blink of an eye, she took off and flew up into a tree of *her* choice. She had difficulty reaching the last few feet. Her wings flapping wildly, she grabbed at a branch as she headed back down. I walked over to the tree. There she was, wedged between two small branches, clinging to the branch as if her life depended on it.

I tried to coax her back down. I called her special name. Whistled. Coo-ed. Chipped. Clucked, and whisper sang to her. Nothing worked. She was not letting go of the branch. She looked at me, and then looked at the ground. She blinked, looked around, and held fast. I went out into the yard and fell down. Lying very still, I opened one eye just a crack. She moved her head to see better... But she didn't budge. (It had worked with Hanna.)

A couple birds flew around the tree, checking her out. A pair of Blue jays flew into the clearing. The male was flitting from tree to tree, squawking his dominance. Glory ducked her head, and sat very still. She didn't move. Blue jays are bullies, pure and simple. The jay noticed me, and decided to move on. He swooped towards the female jay, and they both took off towards deeper woods. I've seen bullies in humans too. I've learned that usually when someone is a bully, they have been bullied themselves. Makes you sort of pity that person.

As I walked back over to the tree, I realized that I

couldn't find Glory. I expected to hear her wings flapping if she took off. I sat down in a lawn chair and raised the binoculars that were in the chair pocket. Scanning the branches slowly, looking for a trace of her, I noticed a pale buff, grey, and white patch in the branches. I moved to get a better view. All of a sudden she moved her head and blinked at me. I immediately felt instant pity for her. The bully had scared her stiff. I gritted my teeth. I don't have much respect for bullies. They use scare tactics to get what they want. I looked around the yard, looking for *something* that would help me.

I saw it. There, over by the basement door was an aluminum ladder. I thought back to my childhood and the memory of doves balancing on small ladders for the magician on television. Doves adapt readily to training. After all, Glory had learned to balance on her cage door opening, and fly over to the bed in her room. I have put her on several perch type bars, and she would walk back and forth like she was on my shoulder. Just like Captain Hook's parrot, Polly. And Glory does like crackers, too!

I turned and headed towards the ladder, wondering if she was watching me. I could imagine her little black eyes peeking through the leaves of her hideaway. I knew the ladder was too short before I ever took it over there. The ladder was only twenty feet. She had landed on a branch at least twenty five feet above the ground. My idea seemed far-fetched. Walking over to the garage door, I started to question whether this was right.

Okay, God. Are you trying to tell me that my time with Glory is up? You know I can't leave her out here stranded on a limb too high for her to get down. She can't stay exposed all night. The barn owl that lives in these woods would enjoy her too much. I don't know if I'm ready to give her up...

I took a deep breath of air and held it as I grabbed hold of the rungs on the ladder. Huh...lifting the ladder and turning it parallel with the ground, I walked back towards the tree. The ladder wasn't balanced. It twisted and turned in front of my legs. My leg caught the ladder and it swung back around, making a clanging rattle. The noise echoed through the woods. I'm sure my neighbors could hear that loud clang. I rebalanced the ladder and started again, this time a little slower. The parts of the ladder that held it secure were still rattling as I approached the tree. I was making enough noise for the whole neighborhood to hear, so I reassured myself that Glory knew I was coming close to her also.

As I got within ten feet of the tree, I could see her face. Her eyes were enlarged and looking at the metal ladder heading straight towards her. She squatted down, readying for flight. I talked to her, trying to reassure her that she would be all right. In a blink, that's all it took. One blink and she was no longer on the branch. I watched as she climbed higher, flapping her wings desperately to reach the next branch. And then I could see her flight change. She started turning to the left, and started her long flight downwards, spiraling out of control. She was twisting, and turning, still flapping her wings to gain height. But it was futile. I was standing far enough away from her that I could see that. I wish I had been closer, she might have headed towards my shoulder. That was her safe place. I caught myself holding my breath. She was now just spiraling downwards. Smooth, too fast, she was heading right for the trunk of a hickory tree.

God! Please keep her safe!

She hit a patch of tall grass. I headed towards that grass, looking for movement. I walked up to the grass, looking for her body. I walked to the other side of the grass clump. There, between the grass and the tree trunk was Glory.

I exhaled a long pent up, shaky breath. Glory was standing there, trying to free her spindly legs from the blades of grass clinging to her. It reminded me of a child trying to pull themselves out of a pair of pants with their feet standing on the opposite pants leg. I couldn't help but chuckle when she looked up at me. There was determination in her eyes. She jumped up and freed herself from the last of the clingy blades. Then she took off, running around the tree trunk, looking for an opening. I bent down and scooped her up and held her close to me. She was panting, frightened. She tucked her head, and leaned into me. I started to whisper that she would be all right. Lightly, I stroked her neck and back. She was chipping to me for all she was worth, telling me I'm sure how scary that descent was from the tree. Walking up the driveway, I continued to whisper and coo and reassure her.

By the time I reached the back porch, she raised her head and looked around. Hanna was waiting on the porch, doing her begging dance. I took Glory inside and up to her room. I sat down on the chair and held her. Or, it was more like she sat on my lap and nestled in. A few minutes later, she was squeezing her eyes shut, nodding off. Doctors told us years ago when my son had a traumatic accident that he would fall asleep on the way home from the hospital. He did. I figured that Glory wasn't much different. She had had quite a scare. And now that she was safe, she was going to take a nap. I wonder how many lives a dove has.

July 17, 2012

Glory and Hanna are playing a variation of their Tag, You're it game. I'm sitting on the wing chair, reading. Glory is walking around on the bed, looking at the seeds spread out on the towel. Hanna came running up the stairs into the room. She just barely stopped before she crashed into the bed. She could see Glory looking over the edge of the bed when she was coming upstairs, but as she got closer, she wasn't tall enough to see on the bed. So she jumped up on her back legs and took a quick look to see where the bird was. About the same time, Glory walked to the edge of the bed and looked over. When Glory realized she was just inches away from Hanna's big pearly whites, she did a rapid 180 ° turn on one foot and ran to the center of the bed. When Hanna saw her turn and run, so did Hanna. She turned around and ran around the bed to the other side. The funny thing was, both me, and Glory could see two ears sticking up on the other side of the bed! So, Glory stayed in the middle of the bed, watching the ears. Hanna finally couldn't resist another peek, and jumped up once again. Seeing that Glory was working her way back to my side of the bed, she ran around to be there when Glory got to the edge again. They can do this for almost an hour. I call it "children entertaining themselves." It is funny to watch. And I really think they enjoy it too!

September 22, 2012

This week we had our first revival at my church. It ran from Sunday until Thursday. I planned to attend just to show support to our church, but I ended up coming away with much more. One of the sermons was about having the faith that God would come through for you if you trusted in Him. The speaker, Lonnie Riley, gave several examples. The funny thing was, that morning I drove to Lexington to be with a friend while she had surgery. When we got her home, she told me that her daughter would help me load the material she had given me. I make dresses for mission trips, and she had gotten a bolt of fabric from her place of employment. It was 72 inches wide, by 95 yards long! I could barely lift the bolt of fabric.

That night Lonnie shared with my church how different things were given to his church by people wanting to help. Clothing and roof shingles were just two of the items that had been donated. That brought a smile to my face, thinking of the large bolt of fabric sitting on my dining room floor! He told us how important it is to have faith that whatever God has started, he will complete. We just have to have faith. There have been several new opportunities that have opened up for me, I just need to be patient, and wait for God's timing!

October 2, 2012

Yesterday, I closed the doors to my bedroom and bath so Glory could explore. While she was doing that, I took a quick shower. When I got out of the shower I went in my bedroom and called to Glory. No answer. I walked around the room, looking behind different pieces of furniture. I finally found her. She had nestled down on a grey t-shirt of mine that had fallen to the floor. The color of the t-shirt camouflaged her. Glory likes to sit on soft clothing that tends to be mine…I wonder if she can smell my scent like dogs can?

October 24, 2012

This morning I put on a fleece sweatshirt to stay warm while I took Hanna outside. When I came back inside, I just kept it on. It felt warm. When I put Glory on my shoulder, she walked over and gave me nibbling kisses on my cheek. Then she walked around my shoulder and settled down. When I looked around to check on her, she was nestled in the hood of my sweatshirt!

November 6, 2012

This morning I got up and made preparations to go swim. My plans were to go vote before going to the pool. I packed up my towel and other items that I use at the pool. I went to our local school and stood in the appropriate line (A – L). I signed my name to the line with my name typed underneath. I was given a paper to fill out the blanks, and then I walked over to the ballot box. I let my vote be sucked in by the machine, much like a dollar bill changer, except it was bigger. It spit it back out. The second try the machine took it. I gave the man monitoring the machine a thumb's up, said goodbye, and went out to my truck.

After swimming I went back to my house to change my clothes so I could go to the Medical Clinic training. This is one of the opportunities I was talking about. Our county needs this so badly for the citizens who live here. I'm proud that I have the opportunity to help establish this much needed service. And after the meeting I realized that the other volunteers that attended the meeting were just as motivated as I was.

November 7, 2012

Today, I gave Glory her first bath! I was researching some information about doves when I found a website that told how to take care of them. What a find! I have seen her stand in her water dish in the past. This website explained that doves like very warm water to bathe in. I have tried to give her a bath in the past, but it has been with cool water, and she didn't like it in the least little bit! No wonder. It was the wrong temperature.

When I went in the bathroom and turned on the water, she looked around my neck, down at the running water. When I glanced at her in the mirror, she looked at me as if to say, "What are you doing?" I turned the water off when the sink had about two inches of very warm water in it. When I put my hand up near my shoulder to pick her up, I could feel her dig into my t-shirt with her toenails. She didn't want to get in the sink! In the blink of an eye, she took flight and headed towards the window.

Imagine her surprise, and mine, when I set her down in the water. Hey, wait a minute...this isn't too bad! It's warm...I had my hand on her back so she couldn't try to fly away. Actually, she didn't try to fly away again; she sat down in the water. She looked like a duck, except she wasn't paddling around. She was sort of floating. She looked up at me with her head cocked to one side. She wasn't going anywhere. I gently scooped up some water and poured it over her back. She ducked her head, or more like bobbed it. I was able to cover her entire body. I stayed away from her head. I didn't have the equipment the website recommended for her face.

When I lifted her out of the water, her tail feathers were pretty wet. They were so wet they looked like little spikes. I got a big towel, carried her into the bedroom and wrapped her up in the towel. All that was sticking out was her head. I had made a cowl over her head to trap the warm air so she wouldn't get chilled. Then I carried her to the computer, sat down and looked at another website. This one had several pictures. I looked down at Glory, and she was nodding her head, and her eyes were closed. Every so often I would blow a warm breath over the opening. She stayed in the towel for a half hour. She has come a long way from the scared little fledgling that I pulled out from under the radiator!

November 9, 2012

Driving home tonight from having dinner with a good friend, I had time to reflect on all the good things that happened this week. We had our last meeting for the free medical clinic before it opens. Things are falling into place. This is going to be a good group of people to work with. And our county has needed this for so long! It is evident from all the people that have made appointments. It doesn't really take much to volunteer for a cause you believe in. And it makes your heart feel good!

Remember the uniform fabric that was given to me? I got an email back from Solomon's Porch in Lynch,

Kentucky this afternoon. They gratefully accepted the roll. I look forward to hearing what they use the fabric for.

The website that I looked at yesterday about caring for birds gave me some good news. I learned that doves have a short life span in the wild. One and a half to three years is about their average lifespan. But doves living in captivity as pets can live as long as twenty years! When I read that I felt myself draw a deep breath, and I smiled. I will be blogging about Glory for quite a while.

Thank you Lord!

And then to top it off, this afternoon, a friend sent me an email and offered to edit my manuscript. To help me, with no strings attached? What an amazing day! Things are definitely looking up... as in Heavenwards! I have prayed for months that opportunities would open up for me. You know the old saying, When God closes a door, He opens a window? I think that's happening!

When I walked in the back door tonight, Hanna met me in the kitchen and proceeded to smell me from head to foot. She was checking out who I had been with, and I'm sure she could tell what I had to eat for dinner! Glory is now on my shoulder. She checked out my hairdo, and rearranged it to *her* liking! She is now perched on my right shoulder, *percolating*. That's what I call it when she is content and chirps her little contented chips as she falls asleep. You know how people will yawn when they see other people yawn? All I have to do to Glory is close my eyes s-l-o-w-l-y a couple times, and she's nodding off. Power-of-suggestion? Contentment? Peace...pure and simple. Goodnight all.

November 10, 2012

I was doing some research today on a website a friend sent me. It was a magazine article online from a periodical called Biblical Archaeology Review, The Enduring Symbolism of Doves.[1] After seeing some of the information, I thought it would be beneficial knowledge. The symbol of a dove has been around long before the Hebrew Bible. And because of this long history, through many cultures, the dove has become a powerful symbol of fertility and procreation, peace and navigation, and not least, it became a sign from God. It represented hope that land had been sighted when Noah sent out a dove from the Ark. When the bird returned the third time carrying an olive branch, it told Noah that the waters of the great flood were receding and the land was once again visible on Earth. Because of this sailor's trick to find land, the dove became known as a sign from God.

---

1   Biblical Archaeology Review, *The Enduring Symbolism of Doves*, Dorothy D. Resig, 2-01-2013. http://www.bibicalarchaeology. org/daily/ancient-cultures/daily-life-and-practice/the-enduring-symbolism-of-doves/

The sound of a dove cooing, both beautiful and mournful at the same time, became a symbol to depict the suffering of the people of Judah. Doves also depicted atonement. Whether the person offered the dove through guilt, or after the birth of a child, the dove was growing in its meaning, building many layers to its complicated aura.

The story in the Bible of Jesus's baptism used the dove, which had already become a symbol of the Holy Spirit, to descend on Him after He came up out of the water. The dove was used in Renaissance art to depict the Holy Spirit, such as the dove flying by the Virgin Mary, and in the art of Andy Warhol, when he painted *The Last Supper*. Early Christians used a dove to identify themselves to other followers of Christ.

And then it *hit* me like a bolt of lightning! I had received God's answer many months before. Reading the magazine article had just verified what I had been searching and praying for. Incredible! I was shaking and my arms were covered in goose bumps all within seconds of recognition. Do *you* remember? Can you pinpoint the day? I laughed out loud. Why hadn't I seen it before? His answer to me is on page eighteen. I had said a prayer after I sewed Glory up. I asked God to give me a sign that everything would be okay. I didn't think about it when the bird recovered, I was just thankful that God had healed the bird. It was not until reading the web article that I realized God *had* given me a sign, I just had missed the significance until just now. Wow, am I slow sometimes!

Throughout my life, everything that I ever did, everything that ever happened to me, all were in preparation of this moment in my life. Every good thing, every bad thing, was recorded and filed away for the future. I couldn't be who I am if I had not endured the pain, heartache, and life-threatening "WAKE UP" moments sent from God. God was getting me back on track. It took those life threatening moments to make me become aware and take notice. For this reason I'm writing this. This story is for **God's Glory**! God sent me a little wounded dove to give me encouragement to get me through the time when I have to be patient and wait on God! Let everything happen in its course and it's time.

I just ask one simple thing. If you liked this book, tell a friend about it. Spread the word. Encourage them to read it. I believe through today's technology, this story of Glory can be read around the world!

Discussion Questions

1. What lessons did you learn from this book?

2. Draw a picture to illustrate one of your favorite scenes in the book.

3. What similarities are there between bird and man?

4. Is there a parallel between the person writing the story and what happens to the dove?

5. Pick words that are unfamiliar to you and make a list of vocabulary words to look up. Write the meanings of the new words.

6. What senses does the dove have that are like

humans? Can you name something that is different than a human's?

7. Do some outside research and find out about bird's vision, and their other senses.

8. Are there other animals in the book that display human characteristics?

9. What are some of the things the author learned from taking care of the bird?

10. Make up some of your own questions and share them with the group.

NOTES:

NOTES:

NOTES:

I originally saw this book as a children's book, with simple lessons that Glory and I learned and hand drawn illustrations. My thought was that children would be drawn to Glory, just as I was; that simple lessons could be learned through her adventures. And that might still happen, depending on the response of this book.